Let's Learn About

Lent

Lent is something that followers of Christ have participated in for hundreds of years all over the world.

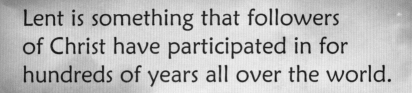

It is a very special time of prayer, of getting right with God, and of preparing for Holy Week and Easter!

Come with me as we take some time to learn more about this very special season.

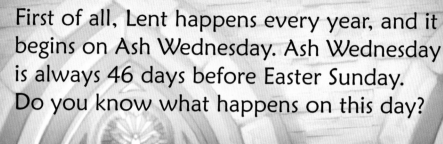

First of all, Lent happens every year, and it begins on Ash Wednesday. Ash Wednesday is always 46 days before Easter Sunday. Do you know what happens on this day?

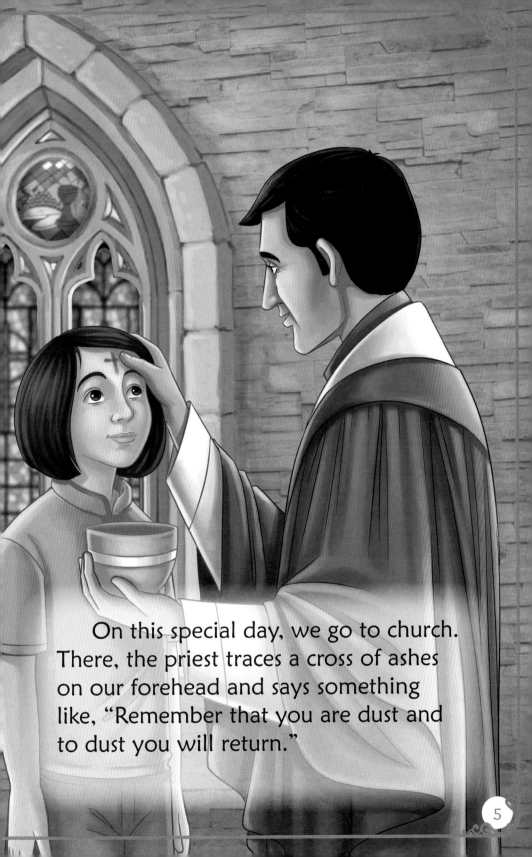

On this special day, we go to church. There, the priest traces a cross of ashes on our forehead and says something like, "Remember that you are dust and to dust you will return."

Have you ever wondered
why we have ashes traced
on our foreheads?

The ashes remind us that one day, when God calls our soul to Heaven, our bodies will return to the earth or to dust. What the priest says also reminds us that God is our creator.

The Bible tells us that God created the first man, Adam, from the dust of the ground. That is why the priest says, "Remember you are dust and to dust you will return."

The ashes also remind us of something else. They remind us that our heart is stained by sin. What is sin?

Sin is when we do things that go against what God wants. Sin keeps us from God and His goodness and brings bad things into our life.

During Lent we pray, "God, if I am doing anything bad or wrong, please show me and help me to change." Lent is a time when we think about our actions, to see if there are things in our life that are not pleasing to God. So how do we do that? Well, we have a wonderful example in Jesus.

When Jesus was going to start the big job that His Father had sent Him to do of bringing salvation to all of us, what do you think He did? The first thing Jesus did after He was baptized was to go away to a desert to pray.

Jesus prayed in the desert for 40 days! The Bible tells us that during that time He was also tempted by the Devil, who was trying to stop Jesus from doing what the Father sent Him to do.

But do you know what happened? Jesus stood strong and when the Devil saw that Jesus was not going to give up His important mission, the Devil had to leave!

The Bible tells us that after that, God sent angels to comfort Jesus.

If God's own Son took that much time to be with His Father and pray, how much more should we?

So, we follow Jesus' example by praying throughout the 40 days of Lent.

Now you may think, *Hmmm. Does that mean I need to go into a desert to pray?*

And the answer is: No! God doesn't expect you to go away to a desert! You can have times of prayer right where you are: at home with your family, and also in church.

And, if you are very, very clever and looking at a calendar you might also wonder, *If Jesus prayed in the desert for 40 days, then why is Lent 46 days from start to finish—from Ash Wednesday to Easter Sunday—and not 40 days?*

And the answer to that question is: because we don't fast or abstain on Sundays, so we don't count the 6 Lenten Sundays.

What is most important during the Lenten season is that we stop our normal activities and take time to think and pray and ask God to show us if there is anything we are doing that is taking us away from Him; if there is any disobedience in our life, any sin.

Why do we do that? So we can ask God for help to turn away from our sin and grow closer to Him!

Being sorry for our sins and turning away from them is called repentance. Repentance means turning around from the way that we are going. It means, if we are doing something that is not good, that we turn around and stop doing it. We stop doing things that displease God.

Did you know that in the Bible, repentance was something that happened a lot? That's because we all need God to help us to turn away from sin.

In the Bible, people would put ashes on their head and wear rough clothing as a way to show they were sorry for their sins—as a way to show repentance. In the same way,

when Lent begins and we have ashes put on our foreheads, we are showing God that we are sorry for our sins, too.

Remember, God tells us to avoid sin for our own good.

It's like a child playing in the kitchen when there is something hot on the stove. A good parent tells the child to be careful or else he or she could get badly burned!

In the same way, God, through His Word and the Church, tells us to avoid sin for our own good, or just like the child in the kitchen, we may get badly hurt.

Sin keeps us from God, and being far from God is not good.

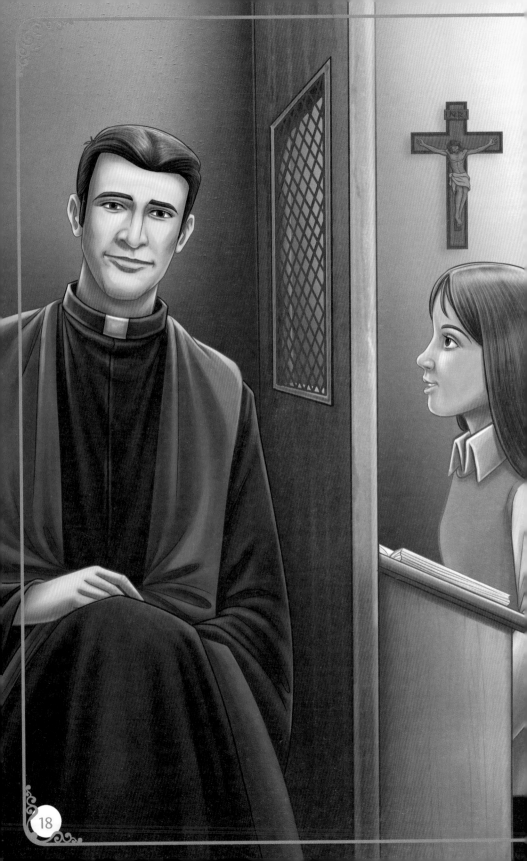

Lent is a time when we think about our actions, to see if there are things in our life that are not pleasing to God and that keep us from being close to Him.

Maybe as we stop to pray, we remember how we sometimes get mad at others or say mean things. Or perhaps we reflect on how we bring trouble on ourselves when we disobey God's teachings.

As we pray, we ask God to show us ways in which we need to change. Then, we go to confession, knowing God will help us.

Do you know what else happens during Lent? Every Catholic, from eighteen to sixty years old, fasts on Ash Wednesday and Good Friday. That means that on those days, we eat only two small meals and one large one, with no snacks in-between.

Also, Catholic families choose not to eat meat on Ash Wednesday, Good Friday, and every Friday during Lent. We might eat fish, cheese or other things instead of meat.

Why do we do that? Well, not eating what we usually like helps us to understand that sometimes we have to let go of what we want to do in order to do what God wants. We call that making a sacrifice.

Now, you might wonder, *why do I need to sacrifice?* It's like training for a sports team. To be good at a sport, you often have to give up doing other things you like in order to have time to practice every day, because if you don't practice you can't be a good player! In the same way, during Lent, we fast or let go of some things we like in order to learn how to be closer to God.

What are some things you can give up during Lent? You might decide to give up watching television and instead, spend that time helping your mom or dad. Or, maybe you'll give up spending money on candy and save it to give to someone in need. Lent is a time when we think about the poor and those who have greater needs than we do.

Be sure to take some time to think and pray about what you will do for Lent before it begins. You may want to talk about it with your parents or the person that takes care of you, so that they can help you!

So, taking time to pray, to repent of our sins, and to sacrifice in order to do good are all things we do during Lent!

During Lent, many churches also have special times of praying together, like praying the Stations of the Cross, which reminds us of how much Jesus loves us!

Lent is a good time to share our love for God together as a faith family, and also with our friends.

Something else really special also happens during Lent: we pray for people who are preparing to enter the Church! As Lent comes to a close, those who want to join the Catholic

Church and have had a time of preparation, studying God's Word and learning how to be a good Catholic, get baptized. This happens during the Easter vigil, which is the night before we celebrate Easter Sunday.

During the vigil, people that have been baptized but have not received the other sacraments of initiation are confirmed and receive the Eucharist. This is a very special and happy time in the Church!

The following day, on Easter Sunday, we celebrate the reason we began Lent in the first place: that Jesus died for our sins and rose from the dead! He made a way for us to go to Heaven, so that one day you and I will be with Him there!

So, why is Lent important, and why do we practice it every year? Lent helps us to be closer to God and better prepared to do His will through prayer; acknowledging and repenting of our sins; giving up things that keep us back from doing His will; and recognizing how much we all need God's help. We can then enter the rest of the year with the power of Jesus in our hearts!

Isn't that wonderful?
I sure think so!

And I hope you have a really blessed Lent!

God bless you!

Go to

www.brotherfrancis.com/lent

and download a free page that will help you in your Lenten journey!

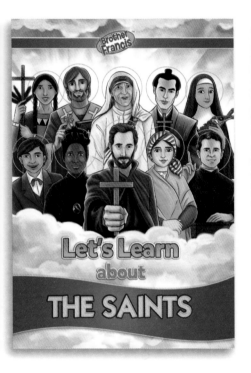

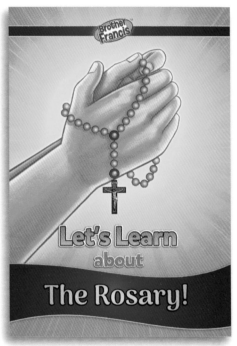

For more books like this one, visit:

www.brotherfrancis.com